Quirky Letters

Faith, Healing, and Honest Words for the Journey

FAITH RAINE

Quirky Letters: Faith, Healing, and Honest Words for the Journey
Copyright © 2025 by MyEsha Eley (Faith Raine)

For permissions or inquiries, contact:
Quirky Letters Publishing
Email: contact@faithraine.com
Website: www.faithraine.com

Book editing, formatting by Lady Brenda Thomas, Book Coach -Warriors Who Write, P.O. Box 124, Beaumont, CA.

www.warriorswhowrite.com

Support@warriorswhowrite.com

ISBN (trade paperback): 979-8-9933506-0-8

Disclaimer

This book is provided for informational and inspirational purposes only. It is not intended to serve as a substitute for professional advice, counseling, therapy, or medical care. Readers are encouraged to seek guidance from qualified professionals for any personal, emotional, or health concerns. The author and publisher disclaim any liability for outcomes that may arise from the use or interpretation of the material contained in this book

Table of Contents

DEDICATION

For every heart that's ever felt broken, lost, or unseen—
this book is for you.

And to my family—my husband, my teenager, my mom and dad,
siblings, and my friends who are more like family—thank you for
reminding me daily that love and laughter can live even in the hardest
seasons.

Most of all, to God, who took every quirky letter, every tear,
and every doubt, and wove them into something
I never imagined: this.

ACKNOWLEDGEMENTS

Writing may feel like a solitary act, but the truth is, I wouldn't have made it here alone.

To my son—thank you for being my reason and my heart. Being your mother has been the honor of a lifetime.

To my husband—thank you for understanding my quirks, moods, and hurt, but loving me through all of them, God blessed me when he sent you.

To my family—thank you for your patience, for giving me the time and space to write, and for cheering me on when I doubted myself. You are the heartbeat behind these words.

To my friends—thank you for listening, for reading drafts, for sending encouragement at just the right time. You've been part of this journey more than you know.

To the readers—whether you've been with me since the very first blog post or you're holding my words for the first time right now, thank you. Your willingness to step into my little world of faith, flaws, and stories is the reason this book exists.

And finally, and most importantly, to God—every page is Yours. Thank You for letting me share a glimpse of what You've been doing in me. May these words bring hope, healing, and a reminder of Your presence to anyone who needs it.

PREFACE

This was never meant to be a book...

It started as scattered words—scribbled in journals, typed in late-night bursts, whispered prayers disguised as poems, and blog posts meant for "just in case someone needed it." I didn't set out to create something polished. I set out to survive, to process, to share pieces of myself with whoever might stumble across them.

But the thing about words is that they don't stay scattered forever. They call to one another, thread themselves into stories, and remind us that even in our quirks and questions, we are not alone.

Quirky Letters is a collection of those moments: brokenness and healing, doubt and faith, grief and laughter, heartbreak and hope. It's messy in places, raw in others, but all of it is real. My prayer is that as you turn these pages, you don't just read my story—you find echoes of your own.

If this book teaches you anything, let it be this: God can take the most ordinary, quirky, imperfect offerings and make them into something beautiful.

So, here it is. My heart, my journey, my quirks—bound together for you.

INTRODUCTION

Welcome to **My World...**

This book is a collection of pieces from my life—letters, poems, reflections, and prayers that I never thought would grow into something bigger. They started as moments: me working through heartbreak, wrestling with faith, laughing at life's quirks, or simply trying to put into words what I felt God whispering to me.

My world isn't perfect. It's messy, complicated, and still very much in progress. But maybe that's why you're here too. Because your world might feel the same way at times—broken in places, beautiful in others, and full of questions you don't always have answers to.

In these pages, you'll find honesty.

You'll find the parts of me that were hurting, the parts that were healing, and the parts that still don't have it all figured out. You'll also find hope, because even in the hardest seasons, God has been faithful.

So, take your time with this book. Let the words sit with you. Highlight, re-read, or set it down and come back later. My prayer is that somewhere in these letters, you'll feel less alone, more encouraged, and reminded that your story—quirks and all—matters.

So, welcome to my world. I'm grateful to share it with you.

—Faith Raine (MyEsha Eley)

PART I
Broken Yet Beloved

*"The Lord is close to the brokenhearted
and saves those who are crushed in spirit."*
—Psalm 34:18

Brokenness has a way of sneaking into our lives.
Sometimes it comes through heartbreak. Sometimes
through church hurt. Sometimes it's the slow, silent
cracks we hide behind a smile. Either way, it leaves us
feeling shattered—like we'll never be whole again.

But here's the truth: broken doesn't mean discarded.
Broken doesn't mean unloved. Even in the most fragile
places of your soul, you are still God's beloved. He
gathers the pieces, not to shame you, but to show His
power to restore.

This part is about being honest with the pain, while also
leaning into the hope that God is near to the
brokenhearted. It's about remembering that even when
our hands can't put the pieces back together, His hands
always can.

Healing and Heartbreak

I don't know what hurts more: heartbreak or church hurt.

What's worse—the betrayal, or the perception of betrayal? Both require us to put our trust in something—or someone—other than God. Both trick us into putting people or things on a pedestal...making them a god at most and an idol at least. And God told us plainly: "You shall have no other gods before Me."

But we're human. We don't always follow directions very well. The truth is, God is infallible. We, however, are not.

So here we are, facing church hurt, heartbreak, and everything that comes with them. I'm not saying we shouldn't trust people. We can. What we should not do is give them the kind of faith that belongs only to God—allowing them to take His place in our hearts and minds. He should be first.

Period.

Full stop.

The problems begin when we forget that simple truth. Slowly—or sometimes quickly—we let flesh take over and push Him aside. And yet, ever the Gentleman, He allows us to learn while staying close, ready to heal us and take His rightful place back in our hearts.

A Tiny Testimony...

I experienced my own heartbreak recently. It was devastating—DEVASTATING. I couldn't eat for almost a week. Everything sent me into crying fits. I was in physical pain, as though I could feel the shattered shards where my heart used to be. It hurt just to breathe.

So, I ran home. To safety. Because home was the only place, I felt I wouldn't drown. But even in that safe space, I was angry. So angry. Angry at the other person. Angry at myself.

Angry at God.

Because how could He—the One who says He loves me—allow something like this to happen? How could He let my heart be broken so deeply? If I'm being honest, I found myself angrier at God than at the betrayal itself.

Does this sound familiar? It's usually how the story goes. And this time, it just happened to be my story.

But here's the truth: God is mending my heart. He is repairing it piece by piece. He's teaching me how to move forward, showing me how to forgive—not only others but also myself. He allowed me to grieve what I lost (something that felt so important at the time), and He forgave me for my anger before I even asked. Still, I asked Him for forgiveness, and for the help to forgive.

He reminded me of His promise:

"No good thing will He withhold from those who walk uprightly."
(Psalm 84:11)

Be it relationship, job, or love—He cannot lie. And right now, He's re-establishing our relationship, making it stronger than before. Psalm 147:3 says He is the mender of broken hearts, and I can testify: **it's true.**

Back to Now...

The tragedy of heartbreak, and church hurt, is that they often drive us away from the very One—and the very place—we need most: God and His presence. We go from relationship to relationship, church to church, searching. Searching for something only He can give.

Or worse—we give up altogether.

Believe me, I know it hurts. I understand the betrayal, the disappointment, the absence when you needed someone most. But hold on. Trust God. Trust His movement—even when you can't see it.

Don't give up on church.

Don't give up on fellowship, or on your brothers and sisters in Christ. Don't give up on God. Because you may be the one He uses to bring healing, not just for yourself, but for someone else. Remember: hurt people hurt people. But healed people can heal others.

Even when you don't want to let go of your hurt, even when you'd rather sit in your anger—you have to release it. As Christians, we must let it go. To heal, we have to set it free, give it to God, and allow Him to do what only He can do.

The God who formed us in our mothers' wombs, who created us in His image, who called us fearfully and wonderfully made—He is the One who can heal the deepest wounds.

A Prayer

Lord,

I ask that You heal us. Take the hurt and replace it with Your peace and comfort. Remind us how highly favored we are, because Your word says so. Help us to forgive those who hurt us—and most importantly, help us forgive ourselves. Take Your rightful place in our hearts. Repair our relationship with You. We thank You for healing, for renewal, and for Your unfailing love. Move on our behalf in every aspect of our lives, and let Your will be done.

In Jesus' mighty name, Amen.

So, with that said—today feels like a good day to start. To let God mend, to heal, to restore what's been broken. The heartbreak. The church hurt.

What do you think? Will you let Him?

The ache of heartbreak isn't just felt in the moment—it seeps into everything. Brokenness doesn't stay in one place; it spreads. And yet, even in that scattering, God is near. Let's talk about what happens when the pieces fall apart.

Fixing Brokenness

Have you ever seen a glass or plate break? It's almost like it happens in slow motion.

The pieces scatter everywhere—under the cabinet, across the rug, smack in the middle of the floor. And somehow, without explanation, one ends up on the counter. The shattering doesn't just stay in one place—it spreads, touching corners you wouldn't expect.

That's what happens to us, too, when we're broken.

Our brokenness spreads into every part of our lives. Our sleep suffers. Friendships feel heavy. Even the smallest things hurt. We try to clean it up, but just like those tiny shards of glass, the pieces aren't easy to pick up. We focus on the big, obvious pieces and miss the small ones—like depression.

And depression is real. It's often the shard we ignore because admitting it feels too hard, after all who really wants to say out loud, *"I'm depressed"*?

Disclaimer: I am not saying depression equals brokenness. I've been there myself, more times than I care to admit. Some days, getting out of bed, and facing the world feels impossible. That's why seeking help—whether it's therapy, counseling, or simply talking to someone—matters.

You are not alone. You are loved. I love you. Christ loves you.

I know it can feel like no one hears you, like the ache will never leave. But hold on. Keep pressing.

> *"When the righteous cry for help, the Lord hears and delivers them out of all their troubles. The Lord is near to the brokenhearted and saves the crushed in spirit. Many are the afflictions of the righteous, but the Lord delivers him out of them all. He keeps all his bones; not one of them is broken."*
> (Psalm 34:17–20)

That's the hope in brokenness: God is near. He hears our cries. He doesn't stand at a distance—He steps in, ready to restore. He tells us,

> *"Come to Me, all who labor and are heavy laden,*
> *and I will give you rest."*
> (Matthew 11:28)

And sometimes, what we need most is simply rest.

There is no shame in seeking help while also trusting God. The two can work together. You can sit with a counselor, take care of your mind and body, and still fully belong to Christ. You don't lose your "Christian-ness" (yes, that's a word now) for asking for help.

Trying to glue the pieces of a shattered plate back together is exhausting. And let's be real—most of the time, we still end up missing pieces. The holes show. The cracks remain. And eventually, we're tempted to just throw it away, convinced we wasted our time trying to fix it.

That's how it feels when we try to fix ourselves without God. The gaps stay. The edges don't line up. And the weight of failure can push us into despair—or even darker thoughts.

But here's the good news: God doesn't just put us back together. He makes us better than before. He fills in the missing spaces with His presence. He takes what was shattered and shapes it into something stronger, something new.

The question is: **will you let Him?**

What the world calls shattered, He calls usable. And every crack becomes proof of His power to restore. Next comes the battle—not with fists, but with faith.

Consumed

~Locked~

Locked...is it locked?

I remember pressing the button but.....
What did I do?
I came in, kicked off my shoes,
started a pot....
But-

Chaos....

Locked!

Shower taken, tv on,
dinner ordered....
But I wonder....
Is it locked?

Think!

Did I press the button?
What did I do?
Okay, one more time
and I swear i'm through....

Locked!

Finally, it's time..
I'm exhausted-
run down...
I just can't remember....
something bad will happen....

Concentrate!

Locked....is it locked?
Just once more....
back outside I go...
This is it, and I promise i'll know...

Locked!

What time is it? 0343....
sleep evades me...
Thoughts consume me,
But there's one roaring louder than the rest....

Locked....is it locked?

Faith steadies us, but the fight leaves scars. Sometimes it feels like we are consumed by the weight of it all. But even in the fire, God shows us He is the greater flame.

Find My Heart

Shattered—

Like broken glass
The pieces stab
Grate....

Pierce—

Slowly embed themselves
Into the remainder of my heart

I can remove the pieces,
Mend the heart
You though,
Have a part

Find me—

Place the last stitch,
Make it right
And hold me tight,
Never let go

But be mindful
I'm battered and bruised,
Scarred and war-torn

Find me,

A whispered promise....
Before letting go
The battered heart,
Clings to hope

Find me,

When you are whole
When it is time,
You will know
Find me,

On the distant shore
Find me
And make my heart whole

In the search for wholeness, we learn surrender. Every lost piece is known by the One who made us. And when He finds our hearts, He teaches us how to fight with faith.

The Letter

I chose a path you cannot take
But I'm not far from thee
I've gone to glory with the Lord
So, don't grieve too long for me

Remember it's okay to laugh,
To even crack a smile,
To tell the stories that embarrassed me-
when I was a child

But if you have to weep that's fine
Just remember to dry your eyes
I'm not as far as you may think
I'm closer than you realize

I'm there in every heartbeat,
Every memory that we shared
Each time we said, "I Love You,"
even if whispered into the air.

I took the path you cannot take
I'm sitting with the Lord
And whenever you start missing me
Just remember these few words:

I loved you then, I love you now
I'll love you ever still.
This is not goodbye my loves.
It's till we meet again.

Loss speaks loudly, but so does love.
Even in goodbye, God whispers of His nearness.
From brokenness, we step into battle—because even
shattered hearts can become strong ones.

Reflection
(Part I: Broken Yet Beloved)

Maybe you've felt it—
the sting of heartbreak,
the ache of betrayal,
the weight of broken trust.

But here's the truth:
your brokenness is not the end.

From Brokenness to Battle

Brokenness can feel final, like the story ends in shattered pieces and unanswered prayers. But God never leaves us in fragments. Every crack, every scar, becomes proof of His power to restore.

And when He restores, He also equips. Broken hearts learn resilience. Broken faith grows roots. Broken people become warriors.

This next section is about that fight—not fists raised, but hearts anchored. Faith that refuses to give up. Faith that whispers "God's got it" when the storm won't stop.

PART II
Faith That Fights

"Fight the good fight of the faith. Take hold of the eternal life to which you were called."
—1 Timothy 6:12

Faith is not for the faint of heart. It's not passive, not quiet background music to life. Faith is active. Faith is a fight. It's choosing to believe when the odds stack up against you. It's holding on when logic says to let go. It's waking up in the morning and whispering, "God's got this," even when nothing around you has changed.

This part is about that fight. The struggle may be real, but so is the God who arms us with strength. Here you'll find stories, lessons, and reminders that faith is more than words—it's endurance. And no matter how small your faith feels, even mustard-seed faith can move mountains.

Funny Little Thing

Faith.

Such a small word, but such a hard thing to live out. By default, we humans are vision-oriented—we want to see it before we can believe it. So how do we believe in something we can't see? On the surface, faith seems almost impossible. Right?

"Faith is the substance of things hoped for
and the evidence of things unseen."
(Hebrews 11:1)

"We live by faith, not by sight."
(2 Corinthians 5:7)

Wait...what?! How can we be expected to believe in what we can't see?

I've always been a little on the curvy side—a plump pillow, chubby, thick, whatever word you want to use. So, when I was told in 2006 that I couldn't enlist in the U.S. Navy because of my weight, I was crushed. That dream felt shattered before it could even begin.

But here's the thing: faith.

Now, don't get me wrong—faith doesn't mean sitting still. What people often miss is that faith without works is dead (James 2:14–26).

I couldn't just say, "I believe I'll lose the weight and join the Navy," then head to McDonald's for a Quarter Pounder with large fries. It doesn't work that way. If it did, I'd be rich by now!

Instead, it meant hitting the gym, watching what I ate, and keeping the faith that God would make a way.

Mustard seed faith.

That's all it takes. Just a little. Like the tiny mustard seed—so small, yet so powerful.

A quick entry about the mustard seed:

Did you know a mustard seed is usually about 1 to 2 millimeters (that's around the size of a pinhead) in diameter? To help paint a picture of this little seed, if you were to line up between 25-30 seeds, they would only stretch about an inch long. To me that's why in the Bible (and in general sayings) the mustard seed gets used as a symbol of something small but mighty — because it's barely visible in your hand, yet it can grow into a plant 6–20 feet tall depending on the variety.

Just like your FAITH!

Anyway, so after **three (3)** exhausting trips to MEPS, the military entrance center, I was worn down, tired, and discouraged. My faith was running on fumes. But I refused to let it die completely.

And because of that tiny bit of faith, in November 2006, God opened the door. Off to Chicago I went, beginning a Navy career as an IT (information systems technician) that lasted until 2015—all because of faith.

The fact is, faith will take you farther than you think. It carried me into the Navy, through years of service, and into a new life after. It blessed me with a healthy child, a civilian career, a vehicle in my own name (that was huge for me), my own place, this very book (my mama told me years ago to start writing this *[spoiler: I didn't listen]*, so: Hi Mom!!), and even the pen name Faith Raine.

God honors faith—even shaky mustard seed sized faith.

Because here's the funny thing about Him: He is no respecter of persons. If He, did it for me, with my sometimes-wobbly belief, He can absolutely do it for you.

Faith doesn't always look like grand moments—it sneaks in, even in small, funny little things that remind us God is still near. But faith is tested in the grind of struggle, where laughter fades and endurance takes center stage.

Fighting to Struggle

The struggle is real.

No seriously—it is. Sometimes it's hard just to lift your head off the pillow in the morning. To take a shower. Fix the kids' breakfast. Brush your teeth. Or even just open your eyes. That little phrase we throw around —*"the struggle is real"*—somehow grew wings and flew around the world. What started as "man, today is kind of rough" became a universal anthem:

"The STRUGGLE is REAL!"

But here's what I can't help but notice: nobody seems to be coming out of the struggle. Am I the only one seeing that?

The Struggle—because at this point it deserves a proper title—has collected more people than I've ever managed to in a game of tag, and it doesn't seem to be slowing down. We all know at least one person who always seems to be the embodiment of "the struggle." In one way or another, they just can't seem to get free. And you're left asking yourself, how?

Here's the truth that might surprise you: struggle is a weapon of spiritual warfare. It's designed to knock us off balance so we never step into the greatness—or even catch the vision of the promises God has for us.

Crazy? Yes. True? Absolutely.

We've all heard it: "No weapon formed against me shall prosper." But struggle is a weapon. And yet, somehow, it prospers—over and over again.

Why? Because we forget that we aren't battling flesh and blood. The problem isn't just that the struggle is real—it's that the fight is real. And that little shift in wording changes everything.

Remember that famous line from The Color Purple, when Sophia (Oprah) says: *"All my life I had to fight!"* Nobody—hear me, nobody— should have to struggle that long. A lifetime is too long to stay in the ring with something God already promised to defeat.

Scripture reminds us:

"The weapons we fight with are not the weapons of the world. On the contrary, they have divine power to demolish strongholds."
(2 Corinthians 10:4)

And again:

"The Lord will fight for you; you need only to be still."
(Exodus 14:14)

So why do we still find ourselves stuck in struggle? Usually for two reasons:

We're using the wrong weapons.

We keep forgetting that God will fight for us—if we'd just step aside.

The problem is, we like to hand Him the struggle but stay in the ring. Then we complain about how rough the fight is while we're still taking hits we were never meant to absorb. It doesn't work like that.

Think wrestling: when you tag your partner in, you leave the ring. You don't stay and keep swinging. But how often do we "tag" God in with our prayers, then keep swinging at the enemy ourselves? (I learned that lesson the hard way, and let me tell you—it hurt.)

Listen—I'm not diminishing your struggle, because it is real. But so is my God. And He will meet you right in the middle of whatever you're facing. He's just waiting for you to step out of the ring so He can fight the battle that was never yours to begin with.

There's no shame in sitting on the sidelines while God does what only He can. You're not quitting—you're trusting. You don't have to fight; you just have to stand. Because the battle is the Lord's.

The fight is real, yes—but so is the harvest. Every battle you survive, every tear you cry, every scar you carry becomes seed in God's hands. Struggles don't end us; they plant something deep within us.

Think about it: seeds only grow when they're buried. And sometimes, God allows our struggle to feel heavy, dark, and hidden—not to destroy us, but to plant us. To take what the enemy meant for harm and turn it into something that will grow roots, push through the soil, and bear fruit in its season.

So as we move forward, let's shift our view: struggle is not just a weapon; it's also a seed. And in God's hands, no seed goes to waste.

Seeds

Matthew 17:20-21:
He replied, "Because you have so little faith. Truly I tell you, if
you have faith as small as a mustard seed, you can say to this
mountain, 'Move from here to there,' and it will move.
Nothing will be impossible for you."

A seed—
Just a mustard seed...

A single mustard seed.
Did anyone stop to think
How small that really is?

How minuscule,
Almost nonexistent,
This little mustard seed.

Not potato, not tomato,
Not barley, nor chia—
Yet this tiny thing
Has the power
To make mountains cower.

With belief...

With faith—

As small as the seed,
The words you speak
Will cause those same mountains
To bow, to heed.

Seeds matter.
Faith is paramount.
The power you need
Is already in the words you speak.
Just believe.

But here's the problem...
Faith is the substance
Of things you cannot see.

And when faith grows faint,
A sad, powerless stillness lingers.

The mountains no longer move.
They don't even sway.

When did we quietly
Put all our seeds away?

Seeds don't grow without pressure. Darkness. Waiting. Our faith works the same way. What God plants in us is tested, and before it grows tall, it often bends under storms.

Before the Storm

It's always quietest right before
the bottom falls out—

That moment just before
the other shoe drops.
When the world holds her breath,
because she knows—

The shoe is falling.
The ground is unsteady.
Lightning is coming,
right after the thunder.

It's in those quiet moments,
waiting for the ground to crumble,
that Silence leans in
and shares her wondrous secrets.

"Run!" she warns.
"Hold fast," she whispers.
"Plant your feet, bend your knees—
if you're trying to survive this disaster."

But then... there are times
when Silence is simply—

Silent.

No advice to be heard.
No answers are given.
All sound muted,
on earth and in heaven.

And it's there, in that stillness,
that I remember
what I've always known:

It's always the quietest
right before the storm.

Storms have a way of making us feel small—
like the sky is too heavy,
the silence too loud,
and the struggle too much to bear.

But storms are also the stage
where God shows up the loudest.
The thunder may shake the ground,
but His voice still speaks louder.

And here's the truth:
the storm isn't the end of your story—
it's just the setting
for God's entrance.

So when the clouds gather,
when the problems line up at your door,
you don't face them alone.

You look them in the eye and say:
"Hi Problems... meet my God."

Hi Problems, Meet God

You wake up. The birds are singing.

Then you roll over and realize—you're late for work. Alarm clock fail.

To top it off: you stub your toe in the shower, then see a note on your front door—rent is late. It gets better. Your car won't start, but thank God for the neighbor who gives you a jump. Then you notice you're sitting on E (you knew you should've gotten gas yesterday). You finally limp into the gas station, swipe your card, and—declined. All you've got is $4.45 in your pocket.

And just when you think it can't get worse, you drag into work and your co-worker Megan (sorry Megan) announces—loudly, in front of the supervisor—that you finally decided to show up today.

Problems.

The saying is true: problems really do have a way of piling up. Suddenly you're sitting at your desk, replaying everything in your head, wondering how much worse it's going to get. Wondering when it will all just be over.

"I pay my tithes," you mumble.

"I go to church," you groan.

"These problems are too much. What am I going to do?" you cry.

Yet not once do we stop and say, "Problems, you may seem big—but I'd like to introduce you to someone bigger."

I've been there too. Wrapped up so tight in my problems that I forgot how big my God was. Forgot that He's the Creator of heaven and earth. Forgot that He is the great "I AM." Everything we are, everything we have, is because of Him. And no matter how fierce the storm, God is always bigger.

This is the same God who said:

> *"Let there be light," and there was light.*
> (Genesis 1:3)

Think about that for a moment. One word, and the entire universe lit up. So how much power can our problems really have when we start speaking His name over them?

In Genesis 18:14, when the Lord was talking to Abraham and Sarah, He asked:

"Is there anything too hard for the Lord?"

Problem: Sarah's age.
God: Sarah gets a baby.
Case closed.

So, when did we stop telling our problems how big our God is? Imagine the peace we'd feel if, instead of spiraling in worry, we reminded ourselves daily: God's got it.

Now, this doesn't mean we won't face trials. Life isn't all sunshine and roses. Sometimes problems come to elevate us. Sometimes they come to teach us. And sometimes, honestly, we create our own storms by stepping outside of God's will. But even then, Paul reminds us:

"We can rejoice, too, when we run into problems and trials, for we know they help us develop endurance."
(Romans 5:3)

That's right—problems help us grow. Mine have. They've taught me stewardship, discernment, prayer, and persistence.

When you don't know what to say in the middle of your struggle, borrow Jeremiah's prayer:

"O Sovereign Lord! You made the heavens and earth by your strong hand and powerful arm. Nothing is too hard for you!"
(Jeremiah 32:17)

No problem is too big for God. He promises:

"I am the Lord, the God of all the peoples of the world. Is anything too hard for me?"
(Jeremiah 32:27)

The answer? No. Unequivocally, unquestionably—NO.
I know this because I've seen Him do it for me.
When I was separated from the military in 2015 (weight control failure—yep, that was my problem), I had no job, no lease, a car payment

and insurance, a child in daycare, bills piling up, and a whole lot of naysayers telling me I wouldn't make it. On top of that, my command flat out said they wouldn't fight for me if I tried to stay.

Problem after problem after problem.

But then I let my problems meet my God. I prayed and cried and prayed some more. And He showed up. He blessed me with an affordable apartment. A job paying more than before. The ability to pay off my car and cover childcare on time. The strength to bring more into the storehouse—gladly and with a cheerful heart.

God showed out.

And if He did it for me, He can and will do it for you.

Scripture says:

"God is not a man, so he does not lie. He is not human, so he does not change his mind. Has he ever spoken and failed to act? Has he ever promised and not carried it through?"
(Numbers 23:19)

And Jesus adds:

"Truly, truly, I say to you, whatever you ask of the Father in my name, he will give it to you"
(John 16:23)

And Jesus can't lie either.

So, here's the truth: problems don't get the final say. They don't get to dictate your peace or steal your joy.

Tell your problems about your God. Then step aside, trust Him, and watch Him work.

Because when God steps in, your problems don't stand a chance.

Every problem has a name. But every problem also has to bow to the Name above all names. This is where faith rises from defense to offense, where battles turn into breakthroughs, and where the fight leads us straight into growth.

Reflection
(Part II: Faith That Fights)

Maybe you've felt it—
the weight of the struggle,
the sting of the battle,
the exhaustion of the fight.

But here's the truth:
your fight is not in vain.

From Battle to Growth

The fight is real. The struggle is heavy. The problems stack higher than the bills on the counter. But here's the thing—every battle we face in faith is also a seed.

Every prayer whispered in the dark, every tear cried into the pillow, every moment we chose to trust God when it would've been easier to quit... it all plants something deep in us. Something that doesn't just survive the storm, but grows stronger because of it.

Seasons change. Struggles pass. But what God builds in us through the battle—that endures. That fruit remains.

Which brings us to the next chapter of this journey: not just fighting, but growing. Because God doesn't just call us to endure; He calls us to flourish.

PART III
Growth & Seasons

"To everything there is a season,
and a time to every purpose under the heaven."
—Ecclesiastes 3:1

Growth doesn't always feel good. In fact, sometimes it hurts more than the battle did. When the storm is over and the silence settles, we're left with the aftermath—the rebuilding, the stretching, the lessons we didn't ask for but desperately need.

The truth is, God works in seasons. Winter doesn't last forever, even when it feels like the cold will never break. Spring always comes, bringing new life in places we thought were dead. Summer shines, filling us with joy and warmth. And autumn reminds us it's okay to let go of what can't stay.

Your life is no different. The fight of faith was not just about survival—it was about preparing you to grow. The seeds planted in your pain, your perseverance, and your prayers? They're about to bloom. This section is about those growing pains, those shifting seasons, and learning to trust God's timing when it looks nothing like our own.

Changing Seasons

You've done this a million times before. You get up, walk to the door, and head toward the stairs.

All you really want is something to drink and maybe a bite to eat. There are twelve steps if you don't count the landing, but this time...

Ten—

Somehow you miss those two little steps.

"This is it. This is how it all ends."

They'll find you at the foot of the stairs in footie pajamas with big yellow duckies on them. And you won't even be around to explain that the pajamas were a gift. Yet somehow—at the very last minute—you're SAFE! But your heart doesn't know that yet.

We get that same "this is it" feeling when we lose friends—or the people we thought were friends. It takes our hearts time to realize we've actually survived the fall. That we're still standing. That we can live to see another day.

The truth is, people come into our lives for three reasons: a moment, a season, or a lifetime.

And let's be real—nobody wants just a "moment" person.

A seasonal person can be okay, because sometimes they grow into lifetime friends. But the ones we all long for are the lifers—the ones who stick through thick and thin. The ones who call you out when you're wrong, celebrate you when you're right, and remain no matter what. The sad truth? There are far more moment and seasonal people than lifetime ones.

Moment people show up to get us through something hard (or sometimes something good), teach us a lesson, and then—poof!—they're gone.

Seasonal people stay longer—months, years even—but eventually that season closes, and they move on. Sometimes they circle back, sometimes not.

Lifetime people—the rarest of all—are the ones we build songs about and write Facebook posts for. They may drift in and out, but deep down, you know they'll always be there.

The hard part? We can't control any of it.

Seasons will shift whether we want them to or not. And that lack of control stirs up anxiety, fear, even heartbreak.

But here's the anchor:

"There is a time for everything, and a season for every activity under the heavens."
(Ecclesiastes 3:1)

And this promise:

"Jesus Christ is the same yesterday and today and forever."
(Hebrews 13:8)

That means while friends and seasons come and go, Jesus is your lifetime. He'll never change on you. He'll never leave. He'll never give you that *"this is it"* drop in your stomach.

So yes—right now, your circle may be shrinking. You may feel like you're losing friends left and right. You may keep "missing stairs." But hold on. Seasons never last forever. And the next one? It will be more beautiful than the one you just left.

Seasons shift. And with every change, we learn something new about ourselves, about others, and about God. But what nobody really says out loud is this: change in your spiritual life can be the hardest of them all. Because when you step into new life with Christ, things don't always get easier— they often get harder.

And that's where the truth comes in: what nobody told you...

Nobody Told You

It's hard when you're young...

And I don't mean young as in a teenager or someone in their early twenties. Sure, those years are tough—full of angst, acne, college, and realizing that life can sometimes just...suck.

I mean it's hard when you're young in Christ. When you're just a babe, freshly saved—or maybe you've been saved for a while, but you're still not quite spiritually mature.

It's hard.

You've done what you were told you were supposed to do:

- ✓ Confessed with your mouth that Jesus is Lord.

- ✓ Believed in your heart that He died for your sins.

- ✓ Tried your best to live a Christian lifestyle.

- ✓ Maybe even got baptized.

So why does it feel like everything got worse? Why does it seem like life is harder now than before?

It almost makes you wonder if it's worth it...right?

But it does get better, beloved. It does!

The truth is: now you're on the devil's radar.

Before, when you were living however you wanted, you weren't a threat. He already had you, and everything you did was profit to his side. But the moment you gave your life to Christ, you stopped being his asset. You became his enemy—and that puts you on his list.

That's what nobody tells you when you get saved: sometimes life feels harder...*at first*.

There's no welcome kit that says:

"Thanks for joining the kingdom! Heads up—it might get bumpy, but keep the faith."

There's no fridge magnet that reads:

"Stay connected to the church. You're on the enemy's radar now."

And no app to remind you:

"It's okay to ask God why things feel so hard."

Disclaimer for the new and the seasoned: Sometimes it's not the devil at all—it's just us. We can't blame everything on Satan. We've got to take accountability. For example:

"The lights got cut off—whew, the devil's been busy!"

But you were two months behind on the bill because you spent the money elsewhere. Or:

"My neighbor tried me today!"

But you've been instigating that neighbor for weeks. That's not spiritual warfare. That's us not being good stewards. That's us not living Christlike. Stop it.

But here's the good news: even though it's hard, it won't always be.

Sometimes the struggles are allowed to draw us closer to God. It's easy to get weary, especially when faith feels new and fragile. But God promised:

"He gives strength to the weary, and to him who lacks might He increases power."
(Isaiah 40:29)

He gives strength. He doesn't leave us hanging. He never leaves or forsakes us.

Faith is what got you here in the first place—believing in your heart, confessing with your mouth. And faith is what will keep you moving forward. You don't need a lot—just a mustard seed's worth.

Things do get easier. Seasons do change.

Change is inevitable, but God never changes. His Word never changes. And if He said it, you can count on it.

One way to help yourself in hard seasons is to find accountability—a "battle buddy" in Christ, as the military calls it. Someone who can pray with you, encourage you, and walk alongside you. Don't try to do this alone. Connect with a church, and most importantly, build a relationship with God. He wants that with you.

Hope is real:

"But those who trust in the Lord will find new strength.
They will soar high on wings like eagles.
They will run and not grow weary.
They will walk and not faint."
(Isaiah 40:31)

That's not a cliché—it's a promise.
If He did it for me, He'll do it for you.
Why? Because He loves you just as much as He loves me.
He already told us:

"Don't be afraid, for I am with you.
Don't be discouraged, for I am your God.
I will strengthen you and help you.
I will hold you up with my victorious right hand."
(Isaiah 41:10)

Life is hard. Being a Christian in today's world can feel even harder.
But with the Lord on our side—we cannot fail.
So hold on. When it gets rough, call on His name.
The Bible tells us:

"The name of the Lord is a strong tower;
the righteous run into it and are safe."
(Proverbs 18:10)

Keep stepping out on faith. It will all work out. Trust God.

It's easy to feel like life is coming at us from every
direction, and sometimes it really is. But other times? The
struggle isn't from the devil, or even from some grand test of
faith—it's from us. Nobody told you this part either:
sometimes, we're sitting in storms we created ourselves.

We Did That to Ourselves

You know that feeling when you knock a cup over?

That sinking, "man, this really sucks, but I did it to myself" kind of feeling. You watch the liquid spread across the table, drip onto the floor, and now you're rushing around to mop it up—only making a bigger mess before it finally starts to look halfway presentable again.

That's a lot like the Christian walk sometimes.

We don't always admit it, but some of the storms we're in? We walked ourselves straight into them.

Most of the time, we want to pin it on the devil. "The devil is trying me." "The devil is busy." But let's be honest: not every storm in your life is the devil's fault. Some of them are yours.

The truth is, we give Satan way too much credit. We blame him for things he never even touched, instead of recognizing the role we played. Sometimes, the storm we're crying about is one we stirred up with our own two hands.

We knocked our own cup over.

So now what?

We find ourselves crying out to God, asking why He would send such a storm, what we did to deserve it—when really, we made this mess. God gives us free will, and with it, we freely make mistakes. Then we turn around and blame Him, or the devil, or everyone else. But sometimes the root of the problem is staring back at us in the mirror.

"For the desires of the flesh are against the Spirit, and the desires of the Spirit are against the flesh, for these are opposed to each other, to keep you from doing the things you want to do."
(Galatians 5:17)

The flesh is fickle. It will lead you astray every single time unless you ask God to help you keep it in check. Otherwise, you'll keep making avoidable messes in your life.

Now hear me—this **doesn't mean** every trial is your fault. God does send tests to refine us. He knows every step we'll take before we even take it (*that's how amazing He is*). But it does mean that some storms are self-made.

And when they are? Thank God for grace and mercy.

Remember that old song? "Your grace and mercy brought me through." Even when we cause our own storms, God doesn't leave us there to drown. He'll chastise us, sure. He'll say, "I told you so." But He will never leave or forsake us. Ever.

That's the beauty of His love:

- No matter the mess.

- No matter how far we've wandered.

- No matter how unlovable we think we are.

- No matter the music we listen to, the backslides we've made, or the mistakes we've piled up.

He loves us. Always. Forever. No matter what.

And when it's all said and done, He picks us up, wipes us off, and sets us back on our feet again. Flesh or no flesh, mess or no mess—He steps into the kitchen, rolls up His sleeves, and helps us clean up the spill.

Because that's the kind of Father He is.

Owning the messes we make isn't easy. It stings to admit, "yeah, I did that to myself." But accountability is where growth starts. And the truth is, once you stop blaming the devil for every cup you've spilled and start letting God deal with your flesh, you begin to stretch into something stronger. That's the hard, holy truth of growing pains.

Growing Pains

The dreaded clothes shopping...

This can either be a great thing—or a horrible experience. Are we going because all that hard work in the gym paid off? Or is it because the only things left in the closet are leggings, sweatpants, and the infamous elastic-waist pants?

Growth works the same way. Sometimes it feels good, like progress you can celebrate. Other times... it just downright sucks. The process itself hurts—sometimes a little, sometimes a lot.

But whether we like it or not, growth is necessary. Spiritually and personally, we can't move forward without change. And usually, growing requires losing something along the way. That loss hurts, but it's not punishment—it's preparation. James 1:3 tells us:

> *"For you know that when your faith is tested, your endurance has a chance to grow."*

Tests are never fun. But if you know what to study for, you're better prepared when they come.

And here's the thing—our "growing pains" often come in the form of everyday struggles. Maybe God starts pruning idols in our lives—those distractions that quietly pulled our eyes off Him. Maybe it's addictions: smoking, drinking, partying. Sometimes it's even friendships or relationships. (I wrote about this in my blog post Changing Seasons.)

These aren't easy to let go of. Quitting habits hurts. Losing people hurts even more. You might find yourself replaying what you could've done differently, thinking if you had just changed one more thing, maybe it would've worked out. That ache? That's the pain of pruning.

But here's the truth: You will be okay. The pain is not permanent—it's proof that you're growing.

We pray things like, "God, Your will be done" or "Remove whatever isn't good for me." And then when He actually does it? We scramble to pick the broken branches back up.

Let it go.

In the words of Frozen—yes, sing it with me: "LET IT GO!"

God never prunes to harm us. He prunes to make room for fruit.

"He cuts off every branch of mine that doesn't produce fruit, and he prunes the branches that do bear fruit so they will produce even more."
(John 15:2)

That means when something or someone falls away, it's not rejection—it's redirection. He's cleaning out what's holding us back and strengthening what's already growing strong.

So here's the choice:

You can leave the fallen branches where they are and embrace the growth—even with its aches. Or... you can scoop those branches into a bag and drag them around, weighed down by what God already said you don't need.

Too many of us are walking around with spiritual suitcases stuffed full of old branches—friendships, jobs, habits, worries—that God already cut loose. And those branches? They're not producing anything anymore.

So what's it gonna be?

Will you embrace the pruning and grow? Or will you keep lugging around the dead weight?

Growth isn't just about what we lose—it's also about what tries to pull us back. And nothing pulls harder than distractions. They sneak in when you're finally getting closer to God, and suddenly the fight isn't about whether you believe—it's about whether you can stay focused.

Distracted by Distractions

You ever notice—nobody bothers you when you're not doing what you're supposed to do?

The truth is, distractions don't show up when you're far from God. They creep in the moment you start drawing closer. The more you lean into His presence, the busier life seems to get. Suddenly, everything demands your attention: people, projects, problems. And before you know it, God has been bumped to the back burner.

That's how distractions work.

They can be anything—relationships, family drama, social media, jobs, even your own storms. Anything that takes your eyes and your time off Him.

And I'll be honest: I've fallen for distractions more than once. Sometimes it feels like a constant balancing act just to keep God first. The good news is, He gives us the ability to recognize distractions for what they are—and the wisdom to stop, pray, and refocus before they drag us too far off course.

Because here's the danger: when we let distractions linger, they become idols.

And idols can be anything we place above God. That's why Scripture reminds us,

"You shall have no other gods before Me."
(Exodus 20:3)

So when life starts pulling you in a hundred directions, pause. Pray. Ask God to clear the clutter in your mind, to clean your heart, and to restore Him to the number one spot.

Distractions will always come—they hunt for us on purpose. But they don't have to win. God's love is steady, constant, unshakable. He deserves His rightful place in our lives.

A Prayer

Dear God,

Thank You for all You do. Please help us to recognize distractions for what they are and give us the strength to stop before we drift too far. Renew our minds, create clean hearts within us, and keep You always first in our lives. Help us to hear Your voice above the noise, to walk in the path You've laid before us, and to focus on You above everything else.

We ask for fresh anointing, deeper relationship, and greater discernment. Thank You in advance for the moves You are about to make in our lives.

In Jesus' name, Amen.

Distractions weigh us down just like baggage does. They pull us away from God's presence, clutter our minds, and keep our hearts scattered. But when we recognize them, surrender them, and let God restore our focus, we find freedom. And that's where we turn next: learning to release what no longer belongs.

Baggage

"Come to me, all of you who are weary and carry heavy burdens, and I will give you rest. Take my yoke upon you. Let me teach you, because I am humble and gentle at heart, and you will find rest for your souls."
—Matthew 11:28–29

When do you get tired?

Tired of being sick and tired.
Tired of being weary and heavy-laden.
Tired of being bogged down,
Dragged down,
Worn down...
Shackled.

Tired.

"Reclaiming my time!"

But not yet—because here comes the luggage.
Do you pick it up?
Of course you do. You always do.

You bring it.
Check it.
Hope it's lost. Pray it's lost.
Then you stand at the carousel... waiting.

"Reclaiming my baggage!"

But just once—
Leave the baggage with the attendant.
Walk past the carousel.
Step back out the door.

Reclaim your joy.
Reclaim your mind.
Reclaim your peace.

Reclaim.

**Baggage weighs you down. The hardest part isn't dropping it—
it's resisting the urge to pick it back up.**

**Freedom is forward. Healing is release. Growth is letting go,
even when your heart misses what's gone. Every glance back
risks a stumble. Every reach back slows you down. God already
cut it off—don't reattach what He removed.**

Eyes ahead. Heart open. Feet steady. Don't look back.

Don't Look Back

Run for your life. If you can't run—speed walk. Either way, move forward and do it quickly. In the military we'd call it: "At a double time, march!" In other words: pick up the pace.

But let's be real—running gets tiring. Sometimes it feels easier to slow down, stop, or worse...turn back.

sigh... You looked back, didn't you?

Do you remember what happened to Lot's wife when she looked back?

> *"But Lot's wife looked back, and she became a pillar of salt."*
> (Genesis 19:26)

Harsh? Maybe. But God had given her a clear instruction: don't look back. And the truth is, looking back always costs us more than we think.

I can't even count how many times I've looked back and ended up stumbling, backsliding, or questioning God altogether. Just like Israel longing for Egypt after God had already parted the Red Sea. They had freedom, yet they craved their comfort zone. And honestly, isn't that us?

We leave a relationship, a habit, or a season that hurt us—but after a few steps forward, we're tempted to run back because the unknown feels scarier than the pain we just escaped. We say, "God, take it away," but then fight to hold on to it.

But Proverbs reminds us:

> *"Trust in the Lord with all your heart and lean not on your own understanding...he will make your paths straight."*
> (Proverbs 3:5-6)

> *"Let your eyes look straight ahead; fix your gaze directly before you...Do not turn to the right or the left."*
> (Proverbs 4:25-27)

The truth is, forward isn't always comfortable.

It can be lonely, uncertain, even painful. But looking back only keeps us trapped. Some people, habits, and places can't go with you into the new season God is calling you to. And no amount of praying, begging, or dragging will change that.

So, keep running. If you stumble, get back up. If you fall, crawl forward if you must. But don't turn around. Don't go back. God is doing a new thing. The future He's calling you to is worth more than the comfort He called you out of.

Forward momentum is the key. So, ask yourself: will you march on—or look back?

Looking back feels safe, but it costs too much. Forward is scary, yes—but it's where freedom lives. Every step ahead is an act of trust, proof that God's new thing is worth more than the comfort He called you out of.

Eyes forward. Feet moving. No turning back.

Reflection
(Part III: Growth & Seasons)

Maybe you've noticed it—
the stretch of change,
the ache of letting go,
the fear of stepping into new.

But here's the truth:
your growth is producing fruit.

From Growing Pains to Encouragement

Growth strips us. It prunes, it cuts, it hurts—yet it prepares. Every loss, every stretch, every uncomfortable shift is proof that God is shaping something greater within us.

But even in the ache, He never leaves us empty. What He removes, He replaces with strength. What feels like breaking, He calls building. And just when you're tempted to give up, He whispers... be encouraged.

PART IV
Encouragement
for the Journey

"Cast all your anxiety on Him because He cares for you."
—1 Peter 5:7

Life is a journey, full of peaks and valleys, laughter and tears. Some days the road feels light, and others it feels like we're carrying the weight of the world just to take one more step. But no matter how uneven the path, we are never walking it alone.

This part is filled with reminders to breathe, to rest, to lean on God's promises when your own strength runs dry. Encouragement is not just "feel good" words—it's the hope of Christ lifting you up when you can't lift yourself. So let this section be your reminder that you are seen, carried, and cared for, even on the hardest days.

With 1 Peter 5:7,
There's Hakuna Matata

Disney had a point.

Okay—let me rephrase that. Disney had a catchy catchphrase. And that's what they do best, right? They give you something sticky— something light and memorable you can sing when you're happy, hum when you're sad, or grab hold of when life feels like it's circling the drain and you need a quick, campy pick-me-up.

Think about it: What means no worries for the rest of your days?

If you said Hakuna Matata, you are 100% Disney-correct...and about 30% real-life correct. Because let's be real—worries happen. Problems happen.

Fall is here, and with this new season come new holidays, new routines, and yes—new worries. Friendships may be shifting, jobs may be starting or ending, news might land in your lap that shakes your heart in ways you can't even process yet. And then comes that person (we all have one...or seven) who says, "Why are you worried? If it were me..."

Are you that person? Please—don't be that person.

So, what do we do with worry? How do we fight something so invisible, yet so heavy?

Because truthfully, worry and anxiety can be paralyzing. They can knock the breath out of you, leave you frozen in place.

Sometimes you don't even know why you're worried, and that's the hardest part—people can't see it, so they dismiss it. But you still feel it.

Jesus said in Matthew 6:34:

"So don't worry about tomorrow, for tomorrow will bring its own worries. Today's trouble is enough for today."

At first glance, that can feel like, Great...now I have today's problems to carry instead of tomorrows. But if you flip it—what Jesus is really saying is: Slow down. One day at a time. Stop sprinting into tomorrow's stress and sit in today's grace. That's not a burden, that's a blessing.

So, let me ask you—have you told God "Thank you" for today?

Because yes, some days the math won't math. There will be more month than money, more bills than balance. I've been there. I know that sting. But even then, God reminds us:

"Therefore, I tell you, do not worry about your life, what you will eat or drink; or about your body, what you will wear...Look at the birds of the air; they do not sow or reap or store away in barns, and yet your heavenly Father feeds them. Are you not much more valuable than they?"
(Matthew 6:25-26)

If He created you in His image, why wouldn't you be more valuable? Why wouldn't He take care of you?

Trust is the antidote to worry. Proverbs tells us, "Trust in the Lord with all your heart and lean not on your own understanding."

That means even when the "why" doesn't make sense—even when friends fall away, interests change, jobs slip through our fingers, or anxiety tries to chain us down—we can still pray:

Lord, no matter what today brings, I trust You with it.

Because He loves us. And nothing He allows is meant to harm us—it's meant to shape us, guide us, and remind us who's really in control.

So yes, worries will come. Anxiety will creep in. Panic might even try to sit on your chest. But that doesn't make you weak, and it doesn't make God smaller. It makes Him greater—and it makes you human.

And if this little campy pep talk isn't enough, go back and revisit Hi Problems, Meet God. Because that's where you'll find the real secret to peace: reminding your problems just how big your God really is.

Hakuna 1 Peter 5:7—it means cast your worries.

It's my problem-free philosophy.

1 Peter 5:7—Hakuna Matata!

Hakuna Matata sounds good on the surface—no worries, no stress. But life doesn't always listen to catchy phrases. Some days the weight presses in, and your spirit starts to ache like your body after a long fall. That's when you realize this isn't about slogans; it's about survival.

It's about knowing where to go when the pain won't stop. It's time to check in—not to a place made by man, but into the presence of the Great Physician.

I'm Here for Check-In

Sometimes, you just need a break.

A time-out of sorts—a chance to clear your head and recharge from the breakneck pace you've been running at. Let's be real: life has been going from 0 to 100 and back again so fast, you're pretty sure you've got a kind of spiritual whiplash. And no, Advil or Aleve won't fix this one.

Is spiritual whiplash real? Maybe not by name, but it sure feels like it.

What you need is a check-in. Not at a fancy resort, not even at a spa. What your soul is craving is a room at the Father, Son, and Holy Ghost Resort & Spa... or better yet, the Holy Trinity Hospital.

On the outside, you smile, hug, and encourage others. But inside? You're sore, bruised, and weary. Your heart feels heavy from being tossed around too much, too fast. You need God to doctor you—and you need Him like yesterday.

There's an old gospel song that says:

"Jesus is my doctor, and He writes out all of my 'scriptions..."

(Yes, 'scriptions, not prescriptions—because when the Seasoned Saints sing it, it just hits different).

And the truth is, God really does give us medicine in His Word—spiritual braces, bandages, and rest to hold us up until He heals us completely.

Jeremiah 29:11 reminds us:

"For I know the plans I have for you," declares the LORD, "plans to prosper you and not to harm you, plans to give you hope and a future."

So no, living weary and broken isn't His plan for you. Healing is. Restoration is. Strength is.

Still... we hurt. We grow tired. We feel worn down.

"My soul is weary with sorrow;
strengthen me according to your word."
(Psalm 119:28)

Even Jesus grew tired. He had to rest. He had to retreat and pray. If the Son of God Himself needed time with the Father, how much more do we?

The Bible is full of "prescriptions" for weary hearts. Here are some worth carrying in your pocket:

"Whoever dwells in the shelter of the Most High
will rest in the shadow of the Almighty."
(Psalm 91:1)

"Come to me, all you who are weary and burdened,
and I will give you rest."
(Matthew 11:28-29)

"...those who hope in the LORD will renew their strength.
They will soar on wings like eagles; they will run and not grow weary;
they will walk and not faint."
(Isaiah 40:31)

"In peace I will both lie down and sleep; for you alone,
O LORD, make me dwell in safety."
(Psalm 4:8)

These aren't just nice verses—they're medicine. God's Word is the brace, the rest, the reminder that healing is already promised.

And yes, it's okay to admit you're tired. It's okay to say, "Lord, I can't carry this anymore." But don't stay weary. Don't unpack and live in brokenness. That's not your home.

Haggai 2:9 promises:

"The glory of this present house will be greater
than the glory of the former house."

In other words, your latter days will be better than your former. Healing is ahead. Restoration is ahead. Peace is ahead.

So maybe it's time to stop trying to hold it all together and check yourself in. Not to a five-star resort, but into God's presence. Let Him take your bruises, your spiritual whiplash, and your hidden weariness.

He's the only doctor who knows exactly how to heal what you can't even put into words.

Unplug for a little while. Rest. Pray. Breathe.

You won't regret it—I promise.

Sometimes, encouragement looks like rest. Other times, it looks like scripture scribbled across stick notes and whispered prayers. But often, it looks like God Himself—our Great Physician—meeting us at "sick call," not with prescriptions from a pharmacy, but with promises that never run out.

Sick Call

I haven't been feeling well....
I do believe I'm sick.
I calmly asked the Doctor,
"Can you write me out a script?"

The Doctor merely smiled,
Then He looked down at His pad.
He lifted up His pen to write...
"These are the writs I have—

For fear, take two: Isaiah 41:10,
Fear not, for I am with you.

Then for anger, take one: Ephesians 4:26,
Don't let anger control you.

If lonely, take three: Deuteronomy 31:8,
He will not leave nor forsake you.

And if tired, take four: Matthew 11:28,
And He will give you rest.

Surprised by the prescriptions,
I still asked for two more.
I didn't speak my issues,
Yet He handed me scripts at the door—

Isaiah 53:5, for your healing:
By His stripes you are healed.
Don't worry about the amount,
Take until you are filled.

And if your faith should fail you,
Use this one right here.
You only need a little—
Just a pinch, if you will.

Matthew 17:20—
Tells you how much you need.
Just a small amount, you see,
Like a mustard seed.

I looked down at the refills,
Noticed they never run out.
Looked up and thanked my Doctor,
And saw my own way out...

The truth is, even when we've prayed, even when we've taken the "prescriptions" of His Word, the battle isn't always outside of us. Sometimes it's inside—our own thoughts that won't quiet down.

Fighting Thoughts

You ever get a song lyric stuck in your head—or a thought that just won't go away?

The kind that sneaks up on you when you're trying to:

- Read your Bible

- Pray

- Talk with God

- Write about your faith

- Basically, do anything spiritual?

You pray it away, or at least try to, but somehow it pops back up later. Like it never really left in the first place.

1. And the truth is, those reoccurring thoughts have an effect:

2. They disrupt your peace.

3. They strain your relationship with God (or at least try to).

4. They either drive you deeper into the Word—or push you away from it.

Recently I heard two things that really stuck with me, and they've changed how I look at these moments.

The first was from a Psalmist who described peace like an atomic bomb.

Think about that: the peace of God is a bomb—<u>an atmosphere-shifting, undeniable force.</u> When it drops, everything around it has to change. Nothing can stand in its way.

That's what Jesus did in the storm. He didn't shout, He didn't panic. He simply said: "Peace, be still." And it was. The storm obeyed.

But when reoccurring thoughts creep in, it feels like they ripple right through that stillness. One small thought can spread like waves in a pond until there's no peace left in sight.

And if we're not careful, those ripples start to pull us away from God. That's why Scripture warns us:

"Keep watch and pray, so that you will not give in to temptation.
For the spirit is willing, but the body is weak."
(Matthew 26:41)

Our minds and our flesh are weak. What we let in through our "gates"—our eyes, ears, and hearts—matters, because it feeds what will eventually come out.

But here's the good news: it's not all doom and gloom.

The second thing I heard came from a preacher explaining Psalm 42:1—

"As the deer pants for streams of water,
so my soul pants for you, my God."

He said (and I am paraphrasing):

This isn't just about thirst. A deer being chased runs to the nearest stream because it knows the water will wash away its scent. Once it reaches the stream, the enemy loses the trail.

That hit me. Because that's exactly how our souls long for God. When we can just reach His presence, the enemy loses the scent. He can't track us there.

Insert praise break.

So, what do we do when those thoughts try to pull us under?

We run to Him. We let the water cover us. We replace the thoughts with truth.

Paul told us how:

"Fix your thoughts on what is true, and honorable, and right,
and pure, and lovely, and admirable. Think about things
that are excellent and worthy of praise."
(Philippians 4:8-9)

When the thoughts come, replace them:

- If a lyric won't leave your head, sing a hymn or gospel song.

- If a negative thought creeps in, counter it with gratitude: "Thank You for breath in my lungs. Thank You for another day."

- If temptation whispers, drown it out with praise.

Because the truth is, God's peace is stronger than any ripple. His presence is stronger than any thought. And the enemy can't track us once we're covered in Him.

Winning the battle in our minds is one step. But sometimes, even when the thoughts quiet down, our hearts slowly start to drift. Not with a loud rebellion, but with a quiet shift—sliding God out of first place without even realizing it. That's when life creeps in, and suddenly He's on the backburner.

Life and the Backburner

Life happens.

It pulls us in a dozen directions at once. We put things off, stop doing what we used to, and let important priorities slide. Or, as my mother used to say, we put them "on the backburner."

But how often do we put God there?

More often than we want to admit.

It usually goes like this:

> Things get bad. Really bad. Bills pile up. A diagnosis rocks you. A relationship breaks down. The job gets shaky—or disappears altogether. The storm is raging, the winds are howling, and you're seasick with no way to steady the boat.

Finally, you call out: ***"Lord, I need You! Please help me!"***

And He does.

In gratitude, you promise to get it together. You show up at church. Dust off your Bible. Reconnect with a faith community. You start to feel new—whole—anchored again. For a while, you and God are inseparable. Like white on rice. Like Frick and Frat.

A real relationship forms.

But here's the thing about relationships: they only grow if you maintain them.

When life smooths out, it's easy to tell God, "I'll drive from here." Even though we don't know where the car is going—or how to avoid another crash.

I've made that mistake myself.

James 4:17 warns us:

"Remember, it is sin to know what you ought to do and then not do it."

Still, we convince ourselves we know better. That the rules don't fully apply to us.

Here's a little story:

I was in a hard season and drawing closer to God. I prayed more. Studied more. The Holy Spirit spoke clearly. My writing flowed. I felt seen, heard, cared for. Then, I made changes. I decided my way was better than His. I prayed "Your will be done"—while pushing for my own outcome anyway.

And slowly, the shift happened. My prayer life dulled. My study time lessened. His voice got quieter. Until eventually, I couldn't hear Him at all.

It wasn't that He left me.

It was that I put Him on the backburner.

The truth is, God never steps away from us—we step away from Him.

And when you've experienced closeness with Him, you feel it when it's gone. You know something's missing. Your spirit aches for it.

Jesus said:

"Remain in me, and I will remain in you. For a branch cannot produce fruit if it is severed from the vine...apart from me you can do nothing."
(John 15:4-5)

That's what happens when we put Him aside. We cut ourselves off from the very source of life.

But here's the good news: even when we wander, He doesn't. Numbers 23:19 reminds us:

"God is not a man, so he does not lie.
He is not human, so he does not change his mind.
Has he ever spoken and failed to act?
Has he ever promised and not carried it through?"

He doesn't walk away. He doesn't change His mind. He waits—patiently, lovingly—for us to return.

Like the prodigal son, He's ready to welcome us back.

So let me encourage you: don't leave Him on the backburner. Bring Him back to the front where He belongs. No matter how far you've drifted, He's still right there, waiting.

Because life will always happen. But so will grace.

The truth is, God never walks away—we do. And the more we choose our way over His, the more our flesh takes control. That's why staying close to Him isn't just about avoiding distractions—it's about daily surrender. Because our flesh won't die quietly. It has to be laid down, again and again.

My Flesh

Daily, my flesh dies.
It cries,
Sings... sighs...
The flesh tries—

And lies.

Daily, my flesh lies
Upon the altar of life.

And I pray,
Fix it.
Make it better.
For it is weak,
And I was told we must die—

Die to it daily.

So daily, it dies,
And daily, it's molded.

Mold it, Lord—
For my flesh is clay:
Malleable, yet sturdy.

What You are making,
I know not.
But I feel the shift,
The breaking,
The rearranging.

Growing pains

That cannot be stopped.
My flesh died again today,
On my knees as I prayed.

In its place,
A holy exchange.
I cannot say I miss it—
My original flesh,
Changed since conception,
Now surrendered,
To be molded by Your direction.

**Dying to the flesh isn't easy, but it clears space.
When the old is laid down, God begins to fill us up—
not with what we crave, but with what truly sustains.
Some cups He empties, others He overflows.
And sometimes, the people around us show us whether
we're being poured into, or quietly drained.**

**The next step on this journey is learning to see the
difference—between what nourishes the soul and what
only pokes holes in the vessel.**

Cups and Bubble People

Sometimes you're just...empty.

Like a cup left in the sink too long, stale with residue. Or like staring out across a horizon that stretches endlessly, with nothing in sight but waves.

Or maybe it's not that you are empty, but that you feel empty—like there's nothing left to pull from, nothing left to give. That doesn't mean you've given up. Far from it—you're a fighter. You've pulled yourself through storms before, and you keep telling yourself that a little sleep, some coffee, and a good long cry will fix it.

Right? Well...hopefully.

You smile. You show up. You say the right words. But even in a crowd, you feel alone. That's the strangest kind of loneliness—being surrounded, yet unseen. Being included, but never quite belonging. And the longer it goes on, the heavier the emptiness becomes.

Here's the bare truth: feeling lonely and empty hurts. It gnaws at you in quiet ways. It whispers that no one would notice if you cried, if you left, if you disappeared. It feels a lot like depression—but not the aching sadness. More like disconnection. A bubble. You can see life happening all around you, but you can't touch it. Can't reach it. And that's exhausting.

David knew this feeling when he prayed:

"Turn to me and have mercy on me, because I am lonely and hurting."
(Psalm 25:16)

Sometimes that's all we can do—cry out. God already knows, but something shifts when we say it out loud. Pretending keeps us stuck; confessing opens the door to healing.

Because truth is—you can't pour fresh water into a dirty cup. You can try, but the residue will always taint what's new. That's why God asks us to hand Him our emptiness, our loneliness, our "leftover mess." He wants to clean and refill us with Himself.

And when the loneliness feels suffocating, His Word reminds us:

"The Lord himself goes before you and will be with you; he will never leave you nor forsake you. Do not be afraid; do not be discouraged."
(Deuteronomy 31:8)

"So do not fear, for I am with you; do not be dismayed,
for I am your God. I will strengthen you and help you;
I will uphold you with my righteous right hand."
(Isaiah 41:10)

"Peace I leave with you; my peace I give you. I do not give to you as the world gives. Do not let your hearts be troubled and do not be afraid."
(John 14:27)

When you hold on to those promises, you realize: you're not as alone as you feel.

I know your mind may still say, "no one cares." But God does. I do. His Word is unshakable, unchanging, and never returns void. If He said He's with you, He meant it.

So, the next time emptiness threatens to overwhelm you, ask Him to refill your cup. He will. And while the world may walk in and out of your life, remember this unshakable truth:

"I am convinced that nothing can ever separate us from God's love. Neither death nor life, neither angels nor demons, neither our fears for today nor our worries about tomorrow—not even the powers of hell can separate us from God's love."
(Romans 8:38)

You are not alone. Never have been. Never will be.

Emptiness is loud. It echoes, it isolates, it convinces you no one sees you.

But here's the truth: God always sees. He doesn't just notice your empty cup—He promises to refill it, cleanse it, and strengthen it.

The loneliness, the bubble, the silence—it's not forever. You are not abandoned, not discarded, not invisible. His Word already told us: "I will never leave you nor forsake you."

And if the Maker of Heaven and Earth won't leave you, then you can rest assured—you are never truly alone.

So, as we step into the next part of this journey, take this truth with you:

You are seen. You are loved. You are not alone.

Reflection
(Part IV: Encouragement for the Journey)

Maybe you've needed it—
a word of hope,
a reminder of love,
a reason to keep going.

But here's the truth:
you are held and never forgotten.

From Encouragement to Love & Legacy

Encouragement strengthens us in the moment—but love and legacy stretch beyond the moment. What God plants in you was never meant to stop with you. It is meant to flow outward, into relationships, into the words you leave behind, and into the lives you touch long after you've gone.

This part of the journey is not just about being filled; it's about pouring out. It's about the notes you write, the prayers you whisper, the footprints you leave. Because one day, someone will look back at your life and see either fragments of fear or evidence of faith.

So, we turn now—from being encouraged to becoming encouragers. From receiving to giving. From surviving to leaving a mark that points back to Him.

Welcome to Love Letters & Legacies.

PART V
Love Letters & Legacies

"I will pour out my Spirit on your offspring,
and my blessing on your descendants."
—Isaiah 44:3

Love doesn't stop with us. It flows forward—through
family, through friendships, through the ways we pour
into others. The legacies we leave are written in the
hearts we touch, the words we share, and the lives we
impact long after we're gone.

This part is personal. It's letters to those we love and
reflections on the people who've shaped us. It's a
reminder that our faith, our prayers, and even our
struggles are seeds sown into the generations that
follow. Legacies aren't built in grand gestures—they're
built in love lived daily.

Daddy's Girl

He's her first love,
Her first date.
If he's not careful,
Her first heartbreak.

The truth is—
He can do no wrong.
She's been a Daddy's Girl
All along.

Rockin' pigtails to ponytails,
Barbie dolls to high heels.
The only thing that never fails:
She'll always care how Daddy feels.

From graduation to graduation,
Job to job and new locations,
Daddy acts without her asking,
Making sure she's never lacking.

Daddy will always be her first love,
A superhuman hero
With powers from above.

Nothing but the best
For Daddy's Girl.
He'll constantly try to give her the world.

He's her first love,
And her first date—
Hopefully not her first heartbreak.

Love begins in the whispers of home—the lessons, the laughter, the quiet presence of those who shaped us first. Before we can talk about legacies that ripple outward, we must pause to honor the roots that taught us what love looks like up close.

Grandma's Chair

On Grandma's porch, there's an iron chair.
I close my eyes, and she's sitting there,
Head slightly bent, in silent prayer...

When I open them up, she's really there,
Rocking in this front porch chair.

The truth is—
I have no clue how long she's been there,
In this iron sitting chair,
Whispering her fervent plea,
For the angels to guard over me.

I've always known,
Somewhere—
Someone—
Prayed for me,
With a sense of urgency,
With old-time faith and true belief,
Never to quit, never to cease.

Each time I visit,
I spy this chair,
Nonchalantly sitting there,

On the porch without a care,
As if it wasn't filled with prayers.

And now and then she'll stop and sit,
And I'll watch Grandma pray in it.
I always wonder what she says
When she sits out there and prays.

And once everyone has gone inside,
It's now my turn
To give it a try.

I take my seat in Grandma's chair
And thank the Lord that she's still here.

**A father's love teaches strength. A grandmother's love
teaches wisdom. Together, they remind us that legacy isn't
just about what we leave, but about the steady hands that
held us along the way.**

Dear Daughters

I don't have a daughter,
You see, I only have a son.
But there is something you should know,
From one girl to another one.

I know you see the "girls"
On the TV and in magazines,
Showing their rumps, twerking,
Trying to be seen.

Ones who think it's okay
To be called out of their name,
Striving for attention
And some bit of fame.

But daughters, oh daughters,
You are worth so much more.
You can do much,
Much more.

The intelligence you hide
By dumbing yourself down,
Trying to keep those so-called "friends"
Around.

Stop it!
Let them go!

It's way past time for you to show
The beauty, strength, and so much sass,
The things you can do, build, surpass.

Find a good mentor,
Stay in school.
One day you'll see,
They will work for you.

Do more than this generation
Has ever done.
You—yes, you, daughter—
You are the one.

So while I wait for you to realize
All you are worth—
Beauty, smile, brains,
Not of this earth—
Just know, daughters of now,
I am here in your corner,
Praying for you
As hard as I know how.

Love doesn't end with family—it expands into community. The words spoken over daughters, the prayers whispered in chairs, the love passed from fathers to children—all of it weaves into a greater legacy: one that belongs to all of us.

Reflection
(Part V: Love Letters & Legacies)

Maybe you've remembered—
the lessons passed down,
the prayers whispered,
the love that still lingers.

But here's the truth:
your legacy is still being written.

From Love & Legacy to Reflections on Us

Legacies begin with love—passed from fathers, prayed over by grandmothers, and spoken into daughters. But legacies don't just live in the people who came before us; they breathe in the mirror of our own lives. From the stories we inherit, we now turn inward—to reflect on who we are, what we carry, and how God is shaping us.

PART VI
Reflections on Us

"As iron sharpens iron, so one person sharpens another."
—Proverbs 27:17

Reflection without action is just standing still. And when it comes to faith, stillness can slowly drift into distance. We've all had those Sundays where sleep sounded better than service, or where we convinced ourselves we'd "catch up with God later." But the truth is—later doesn't always come. Which brings us to a real conversation: what happens when skipping church becomes a habit, and how do we find our way back?

Got to Stop Skipping Church Day

I thought about church today...

But then I remembered that one time I went to that one church... there was that one person or group...

I was going to go to church today...

But then I thought about how I heard the Pastor of that church wasn't the holiest person and wasn't doing right. And you know—who is he to tell me how to live for God if he can't get right himself?

I was going to go to church today...

But I was tired—

I didn't have the right clothes—

They're just going to judge me anyway—

They're all just hypocrites (the most common excuse)—

I was going to go, but...I can just worship in my own home.

Do any of these sound familiar? Do you ever wonder why church? Honestly, what's the purpose?

TO GET FED!

"Like newborn babies, you must crave pure spiritual milk so that you will grow into a full experience of salvation. Cry out for this nourishment, now that you have had a taste of the Lord's kindness. You are coming to Christ, who is the living cornerstone of God's temple. He was rejected by people, but he was chosen by God for great honor. And you are living stones that God is building into his spiritual temple. What's more, you are his holy priests. Through the mediation of Jesus Christ, you offer spiritual sacrifices that please God."
(1 Peter 2:2-5)

The majority of these excuses are tricks of the devil to keep you from going to church, fellowshipping, gaining the Word, and growing in Christ. Of course, you can do things alone—but why would you, if there is no true foundation?

Think of it like going to the gym.

You're doing things necessary to get spiritually "swole" (big on top)... but you're skipping leg day. By skipping church, your foundation is weak and smaller than it should be.

You're skipping Church Day.

Side Note:

> Of course there are hypocrites (they are EVERYWHERE). But God knows who they are, and they have no Heaven or Hell to put you in—that's God's business. So don't use that as an excuse. It's silly.

Anyhow, while at church last Sunday, my Pastor said something that stuck with me:

"The church is full of hurt people."

Just think about that.

A church full of hurt people. The church is a hospital for those who need healing. And yes, even Pastors need healing. If God is the ultimate healer—not the Pastor, not the Deacons, not the Choir, not the people you think are judging you—then why not go where He is?

Remember: "Where two or three are gathered in My name, there I am in the midst of them."

Another way to look at it is this:

If you're hurting and spiritually bleeding out (from all those battles), why avoid the ER because you're afraid of the other patients being treated? Do you have all the necessary instruments at home?

Probably not.

That's not to say you can't watch Joel Osteen or T.D. Jakes at home. They're good for a quick pick-me-up. But try not to make it a habit full of excuses that keep you from fellowshipping with the Body of Christ.

Hebrews 10:24-25 tells us:

> *"Let us think of ways to motivate one another to acts of love and good works. And let us not neglect our meeting together, as some people do, but encourage one another—especially now that the day of His return is drawing near."*

So why are we running away from church instead of to it?

Hurt people hurt people. And yes, there are hurt people in church. But that shouldn't be an excuse not to go. Romans 10:13 tells us:

"Everyone who calls on the name of the Lord will be saved."

And since most preachers are found in church, wouldn't it make sense to go? You don't have to join the first church you find. Try a few until you find where the Spirit leads you.

Do NOT let the devil stop you from going.

Your blessing is there. Your healing is there. Your increase is there.

Those people you felt were judging you? Maybe they were. Or maybe they just had a bad morning. Or maybe they're hurting and don't realize they're hurting you. Who knows? But honestly—if God is working on them (He is), and God is working on you (He is):

"I am sure that God who began the good work in you will keep on working in you until the day Jesus Christ comes again."
(Philippians 1:6)

Then there's nothing to worry about. You should sit back, lift your hands, and enjoy the service.

Don't go to service for the people, the outfits, or the Pastor (they're fine, but they can't help you in the long run—only Jesus can). There's so much you can experience at church that you'll never get from a TV sermon.

Proverbs 11:14 says:

*"Without wise leadership, a nation falls;
there is safety in having many advisers."*

So go for Jesus. Go for the Holy Spirit. Go for God. Go for the Word. Go for the fellowship (in that order).

Pray for the Pastor, the deacons, the leaders—because they're human and fallible. Keep them uplifted.

Don't miss your blessing and healing by being stubborn and thinking you can do it all on your own. We are the Body of Christ, and I don't know of any body that doesn't need all its parts working together. If it doesn't, it's a broken body.

I don't know why you may not go—or if you do go. And honestly, I sometimes miss a service or Bible study too. (I'm not perfect by a long shot. Please don't believe I am.)

I just ask—please don't let it become a habit.

It's not worth it.

The truth is, the church was never meant to be a place where we hide—it's where we come alive. Yet too often, we sit in the pews or stay home on Sundays, living undercover lives, slipping into the shadows, and convincing ourselves that faith can be private when it was always meant to be lived out loud.

Because God didn't call us to be secret agents in His kingdom. He called us to be lights on a hill, salt of the earth, witnesses in the world. So if we've been playing it safe—quiet, invisible, undercover—it's time to step into the next reminder: your faith was never meant to stay hidden.

Secret Agent Man/Woman

Ever looked around and it seems like everyone is moving fast but you're standing still?

It's like something straight out of a movie. Picture it: the camera pans over, and you walk onto the scene—into a house, a restaurant, wherever—and the world slows down, the lights dim, and a voiceover starts: "I bet you're wondering how I got here...to this place...at this time...with these people...well, yeah. Me too." Or something like that.

That's what it's like when you're trying to live the life of a double agent.

So, at this point you're probably reading this thinking I've gone off the deep end. Life of a double agent—bah! Yet something about that rings true.

It must get tiring being an undercover Christian.

Monday through Saturday no one knows that Jesus Christ is your Lord and Savior, yet Sunday rolls around and #ChurchSelfies and #Blessed are all anyone sees from you.

But here's the truth: loving the Lord is a full-time thing.

Your walk with Jesus is your walk. But it's time to get off the fence. You cannot listen to rap music chock-full of curse words all week (or any music for that matter), then switch to gospel for one day and expect to be taken seriously as a Christian. You can't expect people not to see the hypocrisy.

You cannot be a double agent.

"No one can serve two masters, for either he will hate the one and love the other, or he will be devoted to the one and despise the other. You cannot serve God and money."
(Matthew 6:24)

Now yes, I realize it says you cannot serve God and money. But the part we need to focus on is this: YOU CANNOT SERVE TWO MASTERS.

You can't bat for both teams. Play both offense and defense. You can't turn up for the world all week—cursing, fornicating, gossiping, backbiting, etc.—and then show up hungover on Sunday, giving God three hours of half-hearted attention, and call it balance.

We have to do better. As Christians, as children of Christ, it's imperative that we do better.

We were even told:

"From the same mouth come blessing and cursing. My brothers, these things ought not to be so. Does a spring pour forth from the same opening both fresh and salt water?"
(James 3:10-11)

And:

"Either make the tree good and its fruit good, or make the tree bad and its fruit bad, for the tree is known by its fruit... For out of the abundance of the heart the mouth speaks."
(Matthew 12:33-34)

And of course, everyone's favorite:

"I know your works: you are neither cold nor hot. Would that you were either cold or hot! So, because you are lukewarm, and neither hot nor cold, I will spit you out of my mouth."
(Revelation 3:15-16)

Even though this was originally written to the Church of Laodicea, it still applies to us today. We need to pick a side.

Marvel or DC?

Seriously, I don't mean this to be doom and gloom, but rather eye-opening.

How can I speak about being a double agent? What gives me the right?

I'm a semi-retired one myself (God is still working on me, and I want Him to).

I used to curse like a sailor, listened to music that glorified all the wrong things, and loved a good "turn up" with the latest drink in my hand. But I was also a "Well, I guess it's time for church" person.

Yet the closer I walked with God, the more things began to fall away. Cursing was the first to go—even my friends noticed. The latest rap and rock no longer appealed, while worship made my spirit come alive.

Parties became uncomfortable, so I stopped going. Instead, I found joy in Bible study and New Members Class.

By God's grace, cigarettes no longer hold me, and while I still wrestle with a glass of wine here and there, He's still working on me.

Most importantly—I discovered that nothing compares to the fellowship, worship, and presence of the Lord in His house.

Side Note:

Being completely honest, I know it was nothing but God that broke my addictions. If I still wrestle with something, it's not because He didn't take it away, but because I refuse to let it go. (That's another chapter altogether.)

So now, cue the movie scene: lights dim, camera pans, I stroll in casually. "I bet you're wondering how I got here...a semi-retired double agent. Steadily working my way to full retirement. Gladly willing to help any other agents who want to retire, too."

So—are you ready for retirement? Ready to pick a side? Because honestly, it must be exhausting trying to balance on that fence.

Once we step out of the shadows, we begin to see the truth: faith thrives in community. You weren't designed to move alone, but to move with your "click"—the people God divinely aligns you with for purpose, growth, and accountability.

Because walking boldly in the light doesn't just reveal you; it connects you. And sometimes, the greatest strength you'll find is in knowing you're not running this race by yourself.

Click

~Sometimes we all need a wake up call ~

Click—
Pulled over,
He looked suspicious.
Killed because the fear was vicious,
But don't worry, he deserved it,
The ticket from '93 proves his death was worth it...

Click—
Neck rolling, fingers snapping,
Another show with Black women snapping.
Why must it seem like we're always scheming?
Is building up just a pipe dream then...

Click—
BLM.
No, ALM!
No, we mean BLM, too.
But what about Black-on-Black crime?
Your lives must not matter to you...

Click—
Single-parent homes,
Punishment doesn't fit the crime.
Don't you even realize,
Right before our eyes?

Get it together—
the community becomes one,
Or just like—

Click—
The community is none....

The click lingers— a camera freezing stereotypes, handcuffs snapping shut, a tongue clicking in judgment. But when the noise fades, silence takes its place— a silence heavy with absence, with voices unheard.

And so we step into Voiceless, where the greatest weight isn't in words, but in what's left unsaid.

Voiceless

Do—
You—
See—
Me?

Do you?
Right in front of you,
Speaking to you,
Like a broken, lost puppet.

I sing...
I dance...
I twirl...

I prance—

Oh, the world's a stage.
Cue good old Mr. Cellophane.
Can you see my countenance change?
Notice I wear a mask to play this game?

Can you hear me?

Is there sound when my lips move?
Is it just a whisper into the wind...?
There's vibration in the vocal cords,
I feel my lips forming words...

Yet... voiceless.

Are my screams being stolen?
Is that why you can't hear?
Am I not really voiceless—
The sounds... snatched from the air?

Or maybe...

I'm not saying anything worth hearing.
That's the biggest fear:
Scared of slowly disappearing.
Tell me!
Am I still here?

Yes, this is now the reason...

I may just disappear, but I still wonder:
Can you hear me? Am I really here?

Silence can weigh heavy, leaving us wondering if our voices matter. But sometimes the best way to reclaim our voice is to fill it—with words, with truth, with nourishment for the soul. Because we really are what we eat, and our spirits are hungry.

Reflection
(Part VI: Reflections on Us)

Maybe you've realized—
the power of community,
the weight of silence,
the strength of your own voice.

But here's the truth:
you are seen, you are heard, you matter.

Bonus Content:
One Last Bite

This piece wasn't part of the original plan, but I couldn't resist slipping it in. Think of it as dessert after a full meal—something light and playful, but still nourishing in its own way.

They say you are what you eat, and if that's true, then words have been our feast together. So, before we move into the final letter, here's one last bite for the journey.

Food for Thought

They say—

"You are what you eat,"
And truth is,
I'm still starving....

I'm hungry for
Biblical, Scholarly, Literary
Knowledge—

To me this is food,
The best kind of entrée,
Filling and full-filling,
Becoming my entire being.

My mind a library,
Come walk in the stacks.
The more that I eat,
The more fills my racks.

Overthinker, that's me,
A lover of words.
We are what we eat,
And I'm eating those words.

Like a child at a table
Full of candies for food.

The spiritual knowledge,
Biblical intake on a daily,
Has my spirit man hungry,
Slurping up all I can
Like milk and honey.

Scholarly food
Keeps us on our toes—
Competitive and talented
In ways no one knows.

But literary food
Is like a fluffy dessert,
Enjoyed during leisure,
Can soothe away hurts,
Create lands no one knows.

If I am what I eat,
Then it's easy to see:
I'm a walking library
Dedicated to me.

Words can nourish us. They can fill our minds, shape our spirits, and even become part of who we are. But words don't just live in books or poems—they live in us, in our stories, and in the communities we build together.

That's where the journey leads next: from what we eat and take in, to what we share and pour out. From words on a page to reflections on us.

Food for Thought – Reflection

Maybe you've felt it—
the hunger for truth,
the craving for wisdom,
the joy of words that feed your soul.

But here's the truth:

what you take in will shape what pours out.

From Reflections to Farewell

We've walked through brokenness and battles, wrestled with distractions and doubts, leaned into encouragement, and celebrated love and legacy. We've reflected on faith, community, and the quiet places of our own hearts.

If you've made it this far, then you've seen the thread running through it all: God has been here the whole time. In the cracks. In the questions. In the laughter. In the silence.

This book was never about having all the answers—it's about the journey. A reminder that your story matters, your voice matters, and that healing and hope are possible when we keep moving forward with Him.

So, before I close, let me leave you with one last letter. A letter straight from my heart to yours.

A Letter to You

A letter straight from my heart to yours.

If you've made it this far, I want to pause and simply say: ***Thank You.***

Thank you for picking up this book, for sitting with it, and for letting my words live in your hands and your heart. Whether you read it cover to cover or picked it up piece by piece when you needed it most, the fact that you stayed with me means more than I can ever fully express.

When I started writing, I wasn't aiming for perfect. I wasn't giving you a "how-to manual" or pretending I had all the answers tied neatly with a bow. No—these pages came from my life. Real life. Messy moments, healing moments, funny ones, holy ones. And if you've been reading with open eyes, you've probably seen yourself tucked somewhere between the lines.

Maybe you saw a little of yourself...

- In the heartbreak and healing of **Part I**
- In the battles you've fought in **Part II**
- In the stretch and ache of growing in **Part III**
- In the encouragement that breathed life in **Part IV**
- In the love and legacy of **Part V**
- In the reflections of **Part** VI, whispering: *"Yeah...that's me too."*

Or maybe none of these fit—and that's okay too.

Wherever you found yourself, I hope you also found this: **you are not alone**.

That's the heartbeat of everything I've written here. Loneliness, silence, and doubt will always try to creep in, but God's Word, and the reminder of community, whisper back: you are never by yourself.

You matter.

Your presence matters.

Your story matters.

And if I continue to be real with you: life is going to keep life-ing.

There will still be days when you don't feel enough. Moments when challenges look bigger than your faith. But here's the thing—you've got tools now. You've got language for the weight. You've got scriptures to hold onto when your own words feel too small. You've got reminders of joy, legacy, and encouragement you can carry forward. And whether you realize it or not—you've got people (me included) standing in your corner, cheering you on.

This is not the end of your story. It's not even the end of this story. This book is only the first step, the opening note in a longer song. There's more to say, more to wrestle with, more to celebrate. And if you'll let me, I'll meet you again in the next book, continuing the journey we've started here.

But until then—take these words and live them.

Let them remind you that God is faithful. Let them push you to dream bigger, heal deeper, love harder. Let them nudge you when you feel like giving up or believing the lie that you don't matter. Because you do.

You are seen. You are loved. You are chosen. You are becoming more of who you were always meant to be. And the best part? God's not done yet.

So here's my prayer as you turn this final page: may your heart stay open, may your faith grow stronger, and may your tomorrows be brighter than your yesterdays.

This isn't goodbye—it's just see you soon.

With love and hope always,

MyEsha

Epigraph

Being confident of this, that He who began a good work in you will carry it on to completion until the day of Christ Jesus."

—Philippians 1:6

Special Acknowledgements

To my amazing Pre-Order Supporters—
Before the ink ever touched the page, before the binding held these chapters together, you believed. You caught the vision, felt the heartbeat, and chose to sow into this book before it was even printed.

Your support is more than an early purchase it is a declaration of faith, love, and partnership. Because of you, this dream stepped off the page of possibility and into reality. Because of you, hope has found new wings, and stories of healing and resilience will now reach hearts around the world.

I will never forget the courage, trust, and excitement you poured into this project. You stood in the gap with me, and for that, you will forever hold a special place in my heart and in the legacy of this book.

From the depths of my soul, thank you. You are not just supporters... you are history-makers, light-bearers, and co-authors in the story of transformation.

With all my gratitude and joy,

—Faith Raine (MyEsha Eley)

Pre-Order Supporters

Matthew Eley .... Virginia, USA

Tamara Smith-Thomas .... Virginia, USA

Allison Kennedy.. Ohio, USA

Lauren Branham.. Virginia, USA

Jeanmmaire Drake .... North Carolina, USA

Theresa Howard .... North Carolina, USA

Kelvin Leonard ....Florida, USA

Shatika Gray ....Indiana, USA

Jennifer Grimmage-James... Pennsylvania, USA

Latrviyet Hill... South Carolina, USA

Danielle Lamar .... New York, USA

LaTanya Roane .... North Carolina, USA

Cynthia McCutcheon ....Hawaii, USA

TeAnna George ....Maryland, USA

Ashley Bryant..North Carolina, USA

Aszaleigh Jenkins-Rogers .... Virginia, USA

Terri Tharrington .... South Carolina, USA

Telisha Conklin...Maryland, USA

Juanita George...North Carolina, USA

Tracy O. Jackson .... Virginia, USA

Tiffany Johnson..North Carolina, USA

Ocean Williams.. Virginia, USA

Endia Leary.. Virginia, USA

Brandon Ritze.. Ohio, USA

Angie Denisiuk ....Indiana, USA

Michael Roane...North Carolina, USA

Bianca Brown.. California, USA

Anthony Anderson.. Virginia, USA

About the Author

I'm MyEsha Eley—though some folks know me as Faith Raine. A U.S. Navy Veteran by choice and a Military Brat by birth, I like to call myself "an artistic work in progress." Honestly, I've spent my whole life learning to specialize in everything and nothing at the same time, and writing has become the place where all those pieces finally make sense.

What you'll find in my work isn't polished sermons or scholarly essays. It's poetry, journal pages, Bible-soaked reflections, and random thoughts that sometimes sound like love letters, sometimes like prayers, and sometimes like straight-up "girl, let me tell you." Some people call them "Bible Blogs, maybe?" I just call them the truth—the inner workings of my heart spilled out, hoping you'll see God's hand in your story the way I'm learning to see Him in mine.

Outside of writing, I'm a wife, a proud mom to a teenager who keeps me on my toes, and an active member of Theta Alpha Mu Military Sorority, Inc.—a sisterhood where service and legacy are at the center of everything we do. Pouring into others, mentoring, and reminding the next generation that their voices matter is one of the greatest joys of my life.

I'm also a creative through and through. I read like books are oxygen. I write because words heal. And yes—I game...well because we all need hobbies (Shout out to the community that knows me as XPBoosterBae!) When I'm not behind a screen, you can usually find me in an early morning Pilates class, a late-night PureBarre session, or laughing so loud with family and friends that the whole room joins in.

At my core, I believe in legacy. Every whispered prayer, every story told, every word written has the power to outlive us. That's why this book exists. It's not perfect—neither am I—but it's full of heart, faith, and honesty. My hope is that you find a little of yourself in these pages, and even more, that you find God's fingerprints in the middle of your journey.

And I'll be real with you—I'm still learning, still growing, still letting God write this story. But if you've read this far, then maybe we're walking this road together. And to me, that's the most beautiful part.

www.ingramcontent.com/pod-product-compliance
Lightning Source LLC
Chambersburg PA
CBHW020739130626
46554CB00006B/2063